HAL•LEONARD

WOMEN'S EDITION
VOLUME 16

Disney's FAVORITES

WONDERLAND MUSIC COMPANY, INC.
WALT DISNEY MUSIC COMPANY

ISBN 978-1-4234-0110-0

DISTRIBUTED BY

HAL•LEONARD®
CORPORATION

7777 W. BLUEMOUND RD. P.O. BOX 13819 MILWAUKEE, WI 53213

In Australia Contact:
Hal Leonard Australia Pty. Ltd.
4 Lentara Court
Cheltenham, Victoria, 3192 Australia
Email: ausadmin@halleonard.com

Visit Hal Leonard Online at
www.halleonard.com

CONTENTS

Bibbidi-Bobbidi-Boo
(The Magic Song)

from Walt Disney's CINDERELLA
Words by Jerry Livingston
Music by Mack David and Al Hoffman

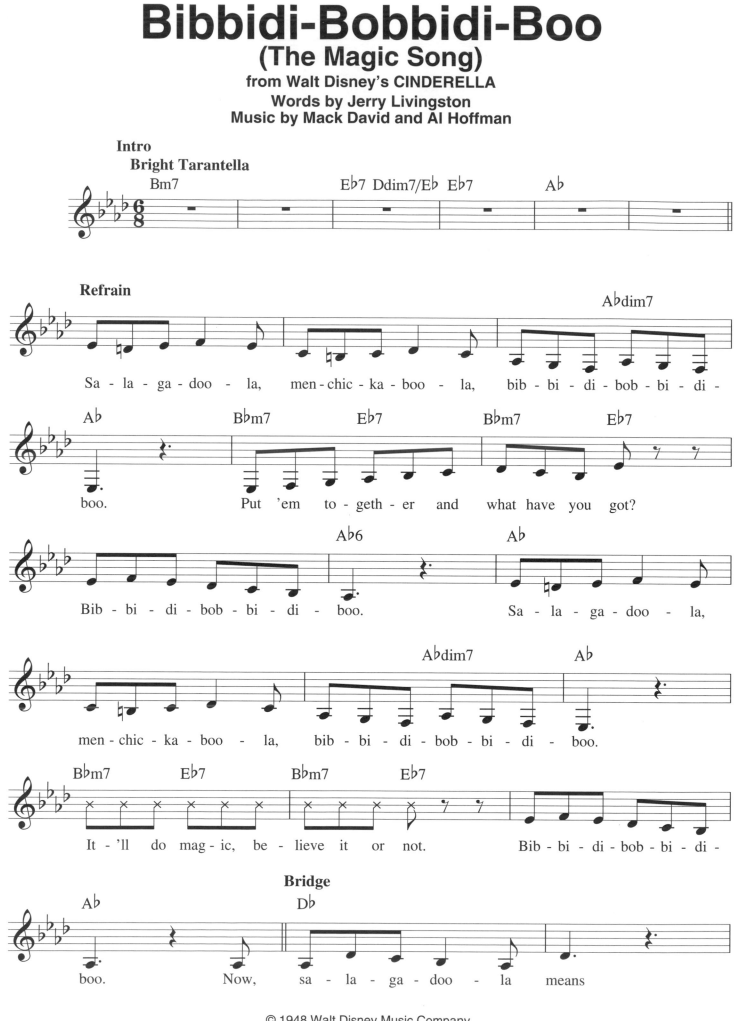

men - chic - ka - boo - le - roo, but the thing - a - ma - bob that does the job is bib - bi - di - bob - bi - di - boo.

Refrain

Si - di - di - doo - doo, doo - de - li - don - da, did - di - li - did - di - li - doo. _____ Doo - bi - di - doo - bi - di, doo doo doo doo, doo - de - li - doo - de - li, doo - de - li - doo - de - li, dee - de - li - doo - de - li - doo!

Outro

Bib - bi - di - bob - bi - di, bib - bi - di - bob - bi - di, bib - bi - di - bob - bi - di - boo.

Can You Feel The Love Tonight

from Walt Disney Pictures' THE LION KING
Music by Elton John
Lyrics by Tim Rice

Intro
Slowly, Calmly

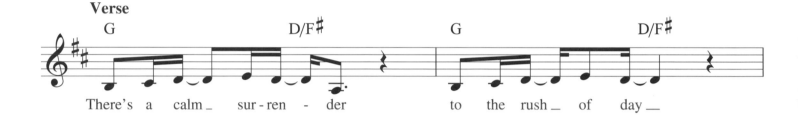

Verse

There's a calm sur-ren-der to the rush of day

when the heat of a roll-in' world can be turned a-way.

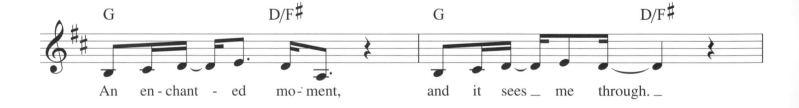

An en-chant-ed mo-ment, and it sees me through.

It's e-nough for this rest-less war-rior just to be with you. And

Chorus

can you feel _ the love ____ to - night? _ It is where _ we _ are. _

_ It's e - nough ____ for this

wide - eyed ____ wan - der - er _____ that we got this far. _

_ And can you feel _ the love ____ to - night, ____

how it's laid ____ to _____ rest? ____

It's e - nough _ to make kings _ and _ vag - a - bonds _ be -

lieve the _____ ver - y best. ____

Interlude

Verse

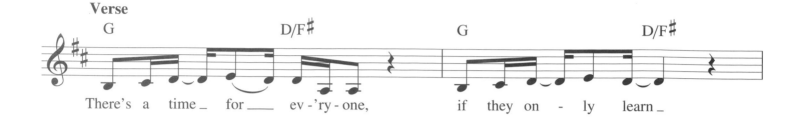

There's a time _ for ___ ev -'ry - one, if they on - ly learn _

that the twist - in' ka - lei - do - scope _ moves us all ___ in turn.

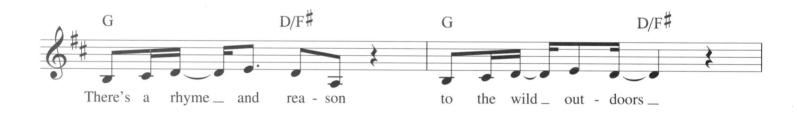

There's a rhyme _ and rea - son to the wild _ out - doors _

when the heart _ of this star - crossed voy - a - ger beats in time _ with yours. _

Chorus

___ And can you feel _ the love ___ to - night? _

It is where _ we _ are. ___ It's e - nough _ for this

wide - eyed ___ wan - der - er ___ that we got this far. ___

___ And can you feel ___ the love ___ to - night, ___

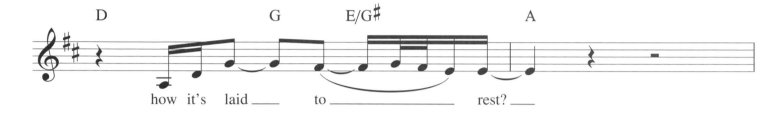

how it's laid ___ to ___ rest? ___

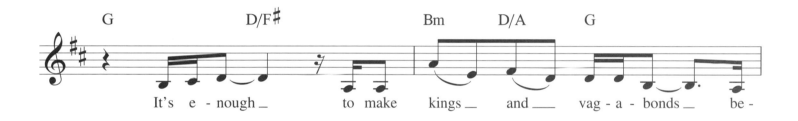

It's e - nough ___ to make kings ___ and ___ vag - a - bonds ___ be -

lieve the ___ ver - y best. ___

Outro

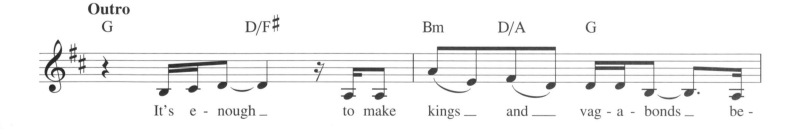

It's e - nough ___ to make kings ___ and ___ vag - a - bonds ___ be -

lieve the ___ ver - y best. ___

A Dream Is A Wish Your Heart Makes

from Walt Disney's CINDERELLA

Words and Music by Mack David, Al Hoffman and Jerry Livingston
(with additional music and lyrics by David Pack)

I Won't Say

(I'm in Love)

from Walt Disney Pictures' HERCULES

Music by Alan Menken
Lyrics by David Zippel

If I Never Knew You
(Love Theme from POCAHONTAS)

from Walt Disney's POCAHONTAS
Music by Alan Menken
Lyrics by Stephen Schwartz

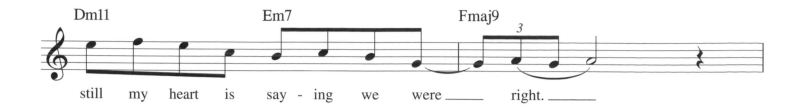

still my heart is say - ing we were _____ right. _____

Verse

If I nev - er knew _____

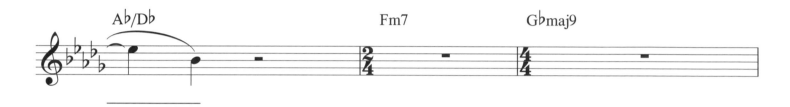

Emp - ty as _____ the sky, _____ nev - er know - ing

why. _____ Lost for - ev - er,

Outro

if I nev - er knew you. _____

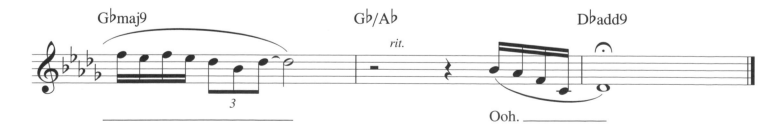

Ooh. _____

Reflection

from Walt Disney Pictures' MULAN
Music by Matthew Wilder
Lyrics by David Zippel

Intro
Simply, gently

F · · · Dm7 · · · C/B♭ · · · B♭ · · · B♭m

Verse

F · · · Dm7 · · · Gm7

Look at me, I will nev-er pass for a per-fect bride ___

C7sus · · · C7 · · · F

or a per-fect daugh-ter. Can it be I'm not

Dm7 · · · E♭9 · · · A♭

meant to play this part? Now I see that if

Fm7 · · · B♭m7

I were tru-ly to be my-self, ___

D♭m6 · · · A♭

I would break my fam-'ly's ___ heart.

A Whole New World

from Walt Disney's ALADDIN

Music by Alan Menken
Lyrics by Tim Rice

Intro
Moderate Ballad

Verse (Male)

Chorus

Eb/F

A whole new

F   F7/A   Bb   F   F#dim7

world,   a daz-zling place I nev-er knew.

Gm   Bbadd9   F/Eb   Bbadd9/D   F/Eb   Bbadd9/D

But now from way up here, it's crys-tal clear that

Gm11   C7   Abadd9   Eb/F   Bbadd9

now I'm in a whole new world with you.

Verse

Dbadd9   Gb/Db   Dbadd9

Un-be-liev-a-ble sights,

Written in the Stars

from Elton John and Tim Rice's AIDA
Music by Elton John
Lyrics by Tim Rice

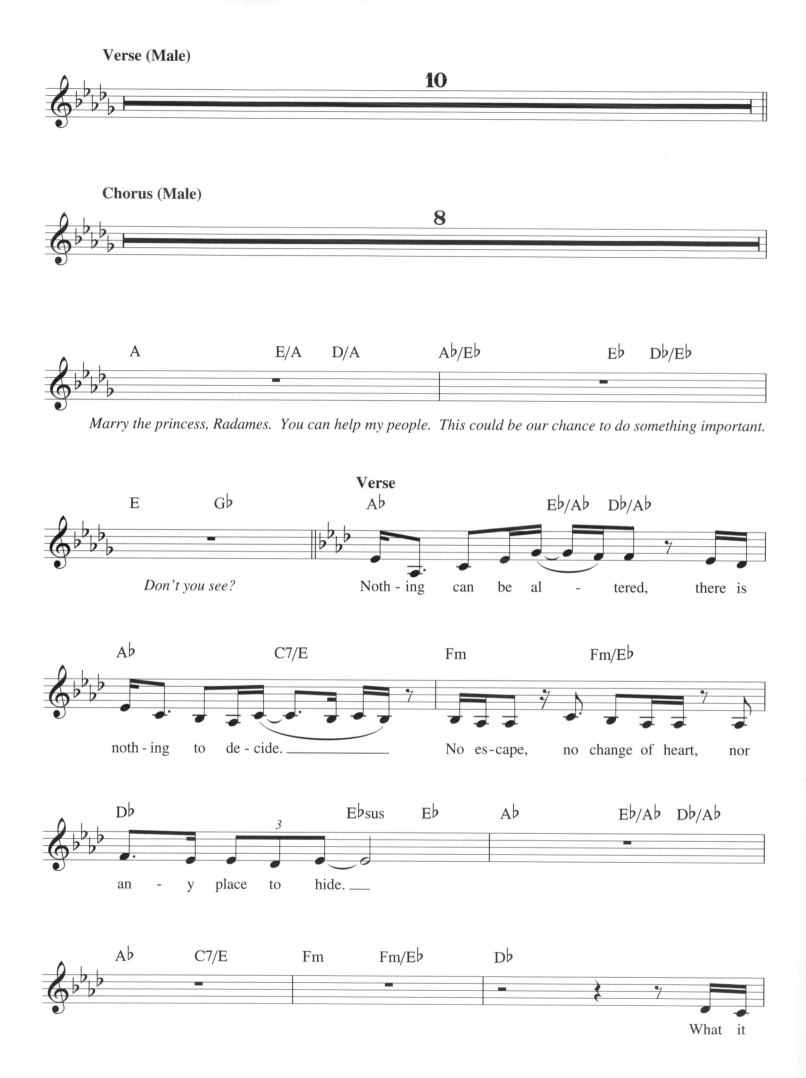

Verse (Male)

10

Chorus (Male)

8

A E/A D/A A♭/E♭ E♭ D♭/E♭

Marry the princess, Radames. You can help my people. This could be our chance to do something important.

Verse

E G♭ A♭ E♭/A♭ D♭/A♭

Don't you see? Noth-ing can be al - tered, there is

A♭ C7/E Fm Fm/E♭

noth-ing to de-cide. _____ No es-cape, no change of heart, nor

D♭ E♭sus E♭ A♭ E♭/A♭ D♭/A♭

an - y place to hide. ___

A♭ C7/E Fm Fm/E♭ D♭

What it

is to be in love, and have that love re-turned. Is it

Chorus

writ-ten in the stars? Are we pay-ing for some crime? Is that

all that we are good for, just some stretch of mor-tal time?

God's ex-per-i-ment, in which we have no say, in

which we're giv-en par-a-dise, but on-ly for a day.

Outro